PIRATES

ANY MAN WHO
DESERTS IN BATTLE
WILL BE PUNISHED
WITH DEATH
OR MAROONING

KINGFISHER

WELCOME TO VS, WHERE THE STAGE IS SET FOR
AN EXTRAVAGANZA OF THE FIERCEST, BLOODIEST,
MOST INCREDIBLE CONTESTS OF ALL TIME.

TEN PIRATES FROM CENTURIES
PAST CLASH AS NEVER BEFORE,
IN FIVE DRAMATIC DUELS...

4 THE PIRATES

THE BATTLES

PRIVATEER
SEA PERSON

BATTLE 1

12 PRIVATEER

SEA PERSON 14

BUCCANEER
CILICIAN

BATTLE 2

22 BUCCANEER

CILICIAN 24

ROUNDSMAN
BALTIC PIRATE

BATTLE 3

32 ROUNDSMAN

BALTIC PIRATE 34

YANG-FEI
FREEBOOTER

VS

BATTLE 4

42 YANG-FEI   FREEBOOTER **44**

BARBARY CORSAIR
VIKING RAIDER

VS

BATTLE 5

52 BARBARY CORSAIR   VIKING RAIDER **54**

WHEN ALL FIVE BATTLES ARE OVER, ONE VICTOR WILL BE CROWNED WITH THE GREATEST HONOUR – HISTORY'S MEANEST PIRATE!

56 FIVE VICTORS

57 THE ULTIMATE PIRATE

58 PIRATE RE-MATCH   **60** PIRATE WORDS

64 INDEX AND CREDITS

NOW LET'S MEET THE TEN GREAT PIRATES ▶

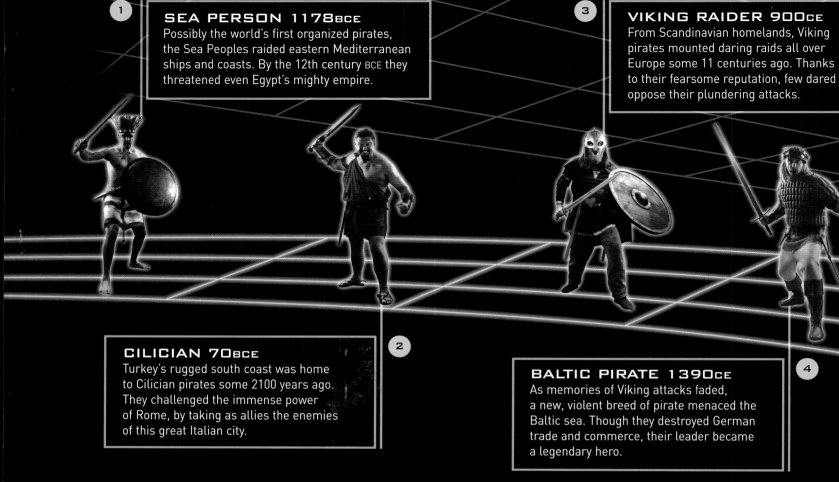

SEA PERSON 1178BCE
Possibly the world's first organized pirates, the Sea Peoples raided eastern Mediterranean ships and coasts. By the 12th century BCE they threatened even Egypt's mighty empire.

VIKING RAIDER 900CE
From Scandinavian homelands, Viking pirates mounted daring raids all over Europe some 11 centuries ago. Thanks to their fearsome reputation, few dared oppose their plundering attacks.

CILICIAN 70BCE
Turkey's rugged south coast was home to Cilician pirates some 2100 years ago. They challenged the immense power of Rome, by taking as allies the enemies of this great Italian city.

BALTIC PIRATE 1390CE
As memories of Viking attacks faded, a new, violent breed of pirate menaced the Baltic sea. Though they destroyed German trade and commerce, their leader became a legendary hero.

LOCATION

PIRATE WORLD
HERE THEY ARE: TEN THIEVING SEA-RUFFIANS WHO WILL FIGHT TO BE CROWNED THE ULTIMATE PIRATE. TIME AND SPACE WON'T STOP THEM: THE OLDEST AND NEWEST MEET AS EQUALS AND THEY COME FROM FAR-FLUNG PARTS OF THE GLOBE. STUDY THEIR COMBATS: PREPARE TO BE AMAZED BY THEIR VALOUR AND SHOCKED BY THEIR GREED AND TREACHERY. CONSULT THE DATA PAGES FOR DETAILS OF SKILLS AND WEAPONS, THEN READ ABOUT THEIR LIVES AND TIMES, AND THE FORCES THAT MADE THEM INTO PIRATES.

PRIVATEER

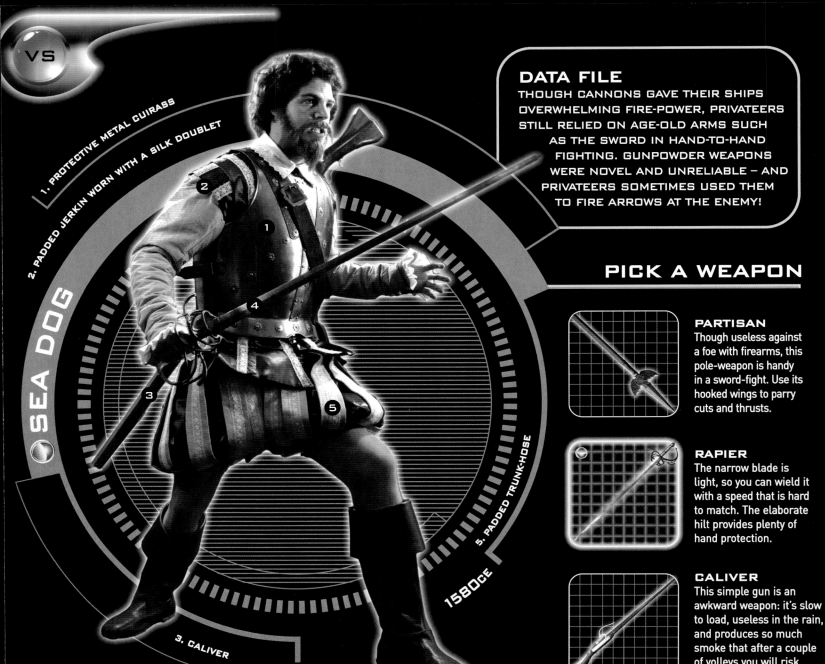

PRIVATEER

SEA DOG

1. PROTECTIVE METAL CUIRASS

2. PADDED JERKIN WORN WITH A SILK DOUBLET

3. CALIVER

4. STEEL RAPIER

5. PADDED TRUNK-HOSE

1580CE

DATA FILE

THOUGH CANNONS GAVE THEIR SHIPS OVERWHELMING FIRE-POWER, PRIVATEERS STILL RELIED ON AGE-OLD ARMS SUCH AS THE SWORD IN HAND-TO-HAND FIGHTING. GUNPOWDER WEAPONS WERE NOVEL AND UNRELIABLE – AND PRIVATEERS SOMETIMES USED THEM TO FIRE ARROWS AT THE ENEMY!

PICK A WEAPON

PARTISAN
Though useless against a foe with firearms, this pole-weapon is handy in a sword-fight. Use its hooked wings to parry cuts and thrusts.

RAPIER
The narrow blade is light, so you can wield it with a speed that is hard to match. The elaborate hilt provides plenty of hand protection.

CALIVER
This simple gun is an awkward weapon: it's slow to load, useless in the rain, and produces so much smoke that after a couple of volleys you will risk losing sight of your target.

ADD STAMINA

FOOD
You should get what you need from raids, but in desperate times be prepared to shred, roast and eat your leather belt and boots!

FIRST AID
If you're bleeding hard, all you can do is tie a scarf round the wound. There's no doctor, so you must rely on your body's healing powers.

ADVICE
If you get downhearted, think of your queen. She shares your hatred of the Spanish foe, and will reward you handsomely for victory.

MAKE YOUR MOVE

AIM...
...And fire carefully! The caliver's flash can singe your beard.

DOMINATE
Your all-steel weapons give you the advantage from the first blow.

THRUST
Your sword works best as a thrusting weapon. Don't slash or hack.

POWER BAR

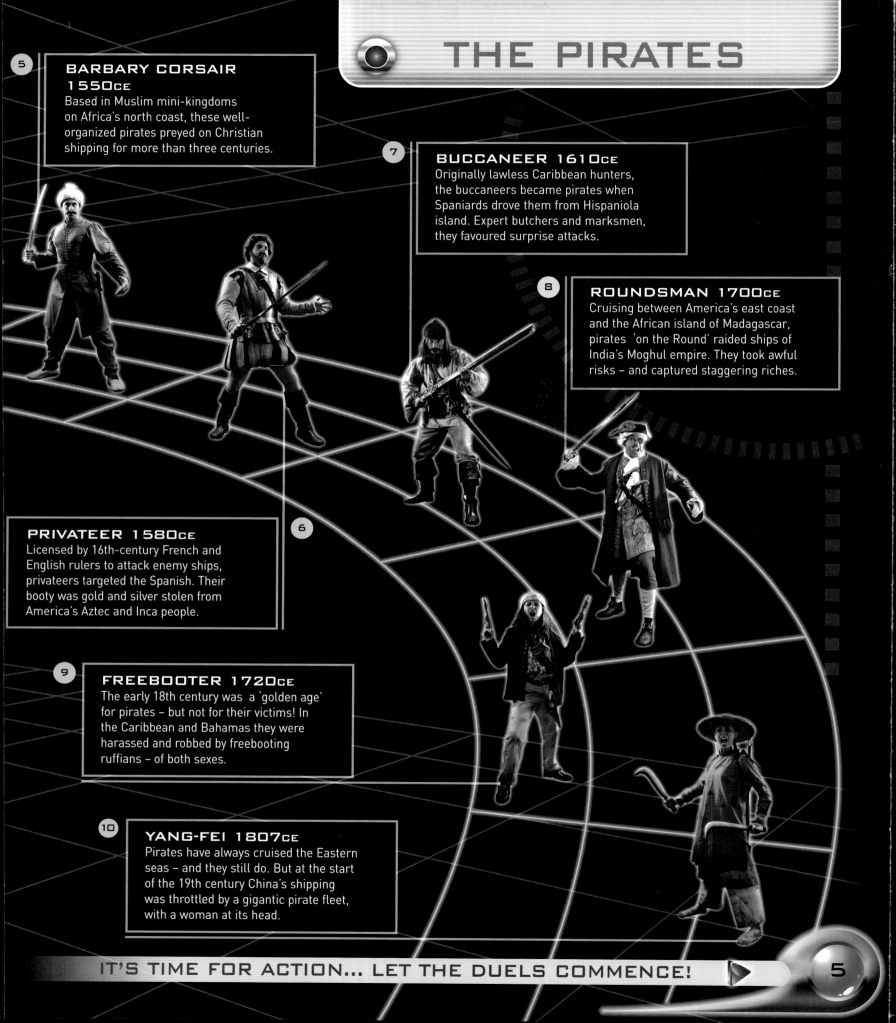

5 **BARBARY CORSAIR 1550CE**
Based in Muslim mini-kingdoms on Africa's north coast, these well-organized pirates preyed on Christian shipping for more than three centuries.

7 **BUCCANEER 1610CE**
Originally lawless Caribbean hunters, the buccaneers became pirates when Spaniards drove them from Hispaniola island. Expert butchers and marksmen, they favoured surprise attacks.

8 **ROUNDSMAN 1700CE**
Cruising between America's east coast and the African island of Madagascar, pirates 'on the Round' raided ships of India's Moghul empire. They took awful risks – and captured staggering riches.

PRIVATEER 1580CE
Licensed by 16th-century French and English rulers to attack enemy ships, privateers targeted the Spanish. Their booty was gold and silver stolen from America's Aztec and Inca people.

6

9 **FREEBOOTER 1720CE**
The early 18th century was a 'golden age' for pirates – but not for their victims! In the Caribbean and Bahamas they were harassed and robbed by freebooting ruffians – of both sexes.

10 **YANG-FEI 1807CE**
Pirates have always cruised the Eastern seas – and they still do. But at the start of the 19th century China's shipping was throttled by a gigantic pirate fleet, with a woman at its head.

IT'S TIME FOR ACTION... LET THE DUELS COMMENCE! ▷

SEA PERSON

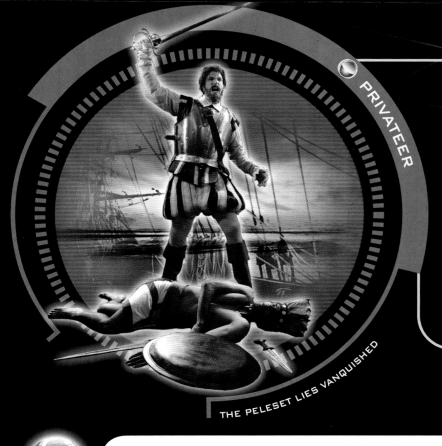

THE PELESET LIES VANQUISHED

THE PRIVATEER WINS

AFTER A FEW MOMENTS OF BATTLE, THE PRIVATEER IS CONFIDENT HE'LL WIN. HE IS A ROUGH SKIRMISHER AND EAGER TO FIGHT. SEA PEOPLE, BY CONTRAST, ARE NOT USED TO PITCHED BATTLES. THE PRIVATEER ALSO BENEFITS FROM 2700 YEARS OF ADVANCE IN METALWORKING. HIS STEEL SWORD IS SHARPER AND HARDER THAN HIS FOE'S BRONZE BLADE. THE SEA WARRIOR MAKES A BRAVE ADVANCE, BUT HIS BLOWS GLANCE OFF THE PRIVATEER'S BREASTPLATE. A COUPLE OF SWIFT, STEELY CUTS LATER HE FALLS DEFEATED AND HUMILIATED.

PRIVATEERS USED WHEELED CANNONS LIKE THIS ONE TO POUND THEIR FOES.

PRIVATEER

BEFORE NATIONS HAD STRONG NAVIES, THEY SENT PRIVATEERS TO FIGHT THEIR SEA BATTLES. WITH ROYAL LICENSES TO ATTACK ENEMY SHIPS, PRIVATEERS MADE PIRACY OFFICIAL – AND THEMSELVES RICH AND FAMOUS.

ELIZABETH WROTE THIS LETTER TO DRAKE, NAMING HIM ADMIRAL OF THE ENGLISH FLEET, IN 1587.

QUEEN OF THE PIRATES
Under England's Queen Elizabeth I (1533–1603, right), privateering flourished. Officially privateers were supposed to carry out raids only to recover cargo or ships an enemy had stolen from them. But Elizabeth knew that privateers were little more than pirates in disguise. She called Drake 'My pirate'.

PRIVATEER'S PRIZES
Spain conquered Mexico's Aztec people in 1521, and Peru's Incas 11 years later. Stolen treasures, such as this gold knife from Peru, were at risk from privateers as galleons brought them back across the Atlantic to Spain.

PRIVATE WARRIORS

England needed privateers to boost her navy, which Elizabeth's father, Henry VIII, started. When Spain sent an Armada (invasion fleet) to England in 1588, the navy depended on armed merchant ships and privateers to repel the attack. Of the ships that defeated the Armada, only one in five was a naval man-of-war.

THIS COMPASS LOST ITS NORTH-POINTING NEEDLE LONG AGO.

NAVIGATOR'S AID

In search of plunder, privateers carried out some epic feats of navigation and endurance. Using only crude instruments such as a magnetic compass like this one, Drake sailed right round the world. The voyage, which took 33 months, was only the second to circle the globe.

IN THIS PORTRAIT, DRAKE LEANS ON A GLOBE, TO SHOW HE SAILED ROUND IT.

GLORIOUS PRIVATEER

The most famous of all the English privateers was Francis Drake (1540–1596). A hero in England, he was loathed as a pirate by the Spanish. When he returned in 1580 from his round-the-world voyage in the *Golden Hind* (below), he brought back an astonishing fortune plundered from Spanish ships and towns. With her half-share the queen paid off all the country's debts, and still had jewels and gold to spare.

AT 37M, DRAKE'S GOLDEN HIND WAS NO LONGER THAN A MODERN OCEAN-GOING YACHT.

FORTUNE AFLOAT

SLAVE BOOTY

In their raids on the Egyptian coast, the Sea Peoples picked out human booty. They could ransom the wealthy, releasing them when their families made fat payments. Other captives they enslaved. However, Egypt was a wealthy nation, and the Sea Peoples would have plundered scent, furniture, chariots, horses, linen, oil, ivory, and precious metals and gems before burning down the towns they attacked.

SEA PERSON

THE WARRIOR RAIDERS WHO ATTACKED EGYPT 3200 YEARS AGO ARE ONE OF PIRACY'S GREAT MYSTERIES. ALMOST ALL WE KNOW ABOUT THEM COMES FROM A MURAL RECORDING THEIR DESTRUCTION.

A COIN FROM PHOENICIA SHOWING A WAR GALLEY

BRONZE WEAPONS

ROWING IN FOR THE ATTACK

The Sea Peoples landed from swift galleys: vessels powered by rows of oars. Though this coin was stamped out some nine centuries later, it shows a similar ship. The main difference is that Sea Peoples' galleys had distinctive 'duck's head' decorations at the front and back.

REPLICA OF SEA PEOPLES' BRONZE SPEAR, SWORD AND DAGGER

PORTRAIT OF A PELESET PIRATE FROM THE MURAL AT MEDINET HABU

A KILT, A SWORD AND A SMART HAT

We know what the Sea People looked like, because the mural at Medinet Habu shows them many times. These ancient pirates fought in elaborate head-dresses, held in place with chin-straps. The crests may have been feathers, but historians have also guessed that they were made of paper, leather, reeds, or even the warriors' own hair, gelled-up in Mohican quiffs!

VENGEFUL RULER

The Sea Peoples met their match in the great Egyptian pharaoh (king) Ramesses III, who ruled the country from 1186 to 1115BCE. In an inscription on the wall of his tomb-temple at Medinet Habu, he brags that he lured them into the mouth of the Nile River. There, in a massive sea-battle, the Egyptian navy massacred them.

PHARAOH HUNTING

The writing on Ramesses' tomb-temple describes how the pharaoh caught the Sea Peoples like 'birds in a net'. The Nile delta where he trapped them was a popular place for hunting and trapping birds and fish. This painting shows wealthy official Nebamun hunting. He stands on a small reed hunting raft that is very like a surf-board.

MAN OF MYSTERY

The Sea Peoples began raiding around the 20th century BCE, but it was 700 years before they became a real problem for Egypt. We don't know exactly who they were, but experts believe that their homelands were spread around the eastern end of the Mediterranean Sea, from southern Turkey to Egypt's northern border. This Sea Person is one of the Peleset, better known by their Bible name: the Philistines.

PELESET WARRIORS FOUGHT IN STRIPED, TASSELLED KILTS.

> " The warriors from the sea islands advanced to Egypt. The net was made ready to ensnare them. Entering into the river-mouth, they fell into it. Caught, they were executed and their bodies stripped. "
>
> Description of the defeat of the Sea People, from the Great Temple at Medinet Habu

CILICIAN

BUCCANEER

THE BUCCANEER WINS

WHEN COMBAT BEGINS, THE CILICIAN DANGEROUSLY MISJUDGES HIS ADVERSARY. HE IS RELIEVED THAT THE OTHER PIRATE'S CUTLASS IS NO LONGER THAN HIS GLADIUS. AND HE GUESSES – CORRECTLY – THAT THE BUCCANEER'S GUN WILL BE USELESS IN CLOSE COMBAT. BUT HE UNDERESTIMATES THE BUCCANEER'S SWORDSMANSHIP, AND RAPIDLY FALLS VICTIM TO ACCURATE SLASHES. SENSING VICTORY, THE BUCCANEER KNOCKS HIS FOE TO THE GROUND, BUT SPARES HIS LIFE. HE CELEBRATES HIS WIN WITH A CLENCHED-FIST SALUTE – AND A STRING OF CURSES!

THE CILICIAN IS DEFEATED

BUCCANEER

STINKING AND STREAKED WITH BLOOD, BUCCANEERS WERE 17TH-CENTURY HUNTER-PIRATES FROM HISPANIOLA. WHEN THEY TIRED OF SELLING MEAT TO PASSING SHIPS, THEY ROBBED THEM INSTEAD.

MANY BUCCANEERS WASTED THEIR BOOTY ON DRINKING AND GAMBLING WITH CARDS.

ATTACKING A TREASURE SHIP

The buccaneers used boats and small ships to sail very close to their targets. Marksmen shot the helmsman and those in the rigging. After jamming the rudder they swarmed aboard, killing any Spaniards among the galleon's crew and passengers. Their raids became bolder after 1630.

PRECIOUS TREASURE

Buccaneers could make a profit from almost any cargo, but they especially prized Spanish coins. The gold doubloon was compact and valuable. The silver 8-real coin – a piece of eight – was almost an international currency. It eventually became the American silver dollar.

ISLAND OF PIRATES

Hispaniola is the Caribbean's second-largest island. The buccaneers left it around 1630 when the Spanish killed all the beasts they had hunted. Intent on revenge, the buccaneers moved to Tortuga (circled). Calling themselves the Bretheren of the Coast, they began brutal, army-style raids on Spanish ships and towns.

FAMOUS BUCCANEERS

A LEGENDARY FRENCH TORTURER

The most brutal buccaneer was a Frenchman nicknamed L'Olonnois (1630–68). He tortured Spaniards he suspected of hiding treasure. Once he cut out a man's beating heart, and chewed on it. After joining the Bretheren of the Coast, L'Olonnois led a ragged army of 1000 pirates.

AN OLD CARIBBEAN BALLAD CALLS THESE ROUGH HUNTERS AND PIRATES 'BLOODY, BLOODY BUCCANEERS'.

WELSH PIRATE TO ISLAND RULER

United by a hatred of Spain, pirates of other nations joined the buccaneers. The most daring was Welshman Henry Morgan (c.1635–88). In 1671 he attacked the city of Panama with 2000 followers. They took little plunder, but Morgan won fame, and a job as Jamaica's governor.

AIMING FOR PLUNDER

French hunters flocked to Hispaniola when Spanish settlers left in 1605. Camping in the island's dense forests, they hunted the cattle and hogs the departing Spanish had released. They smoked the meat on barbecues called boucans, earning themselves the name boucaniers, or buccaneers. Soon, though, they were putting their shooting and butchery skills to more sinister uses as pirates.

THE CILICIAN PIRATE'S MAIN WEAPON: THE GLADIUS

HUMAN PLUNDER

Cilician pirates sold their captives in slave markets on the Greek island of Delos. They were bought by the Roman people of Italy, who relied on slaves to do their dirtiest, hardest jobs. The luckiest slaves worked as house servants, but some fought and died as gladiators. This picture from a 2000 film shows a slave forced to compete as a gladiator.

CILICIAN

FROM TURKISH BASES, CILICIAN PIRATES OF THE FIRST CENTURY BCE RAIDED THE SHIPS AND COASTS OF THE EASTERN MEDITERRANEAN SEA. THEY ENSLAVED THE YOUNG AND BEAUTIFUL THEY CAPTURED, AND MURDERED THE REST.

RANSOMED LEADER

Around 75BCE Cilician pirates seized Julius Caesar, who would later rule Rome. After his family paid a ransom, the pirates released Caesar – who returned, captured them all and crucified them!

> "The pirates' power extended over the whole Mediterranean Sea, making it unnavigable. This was what inclined the Romans to send out Pompey to take the sea away from the pirates. ... Some of the pirate bands begged for mercy."
>
> Plutarch's Life of Pompey

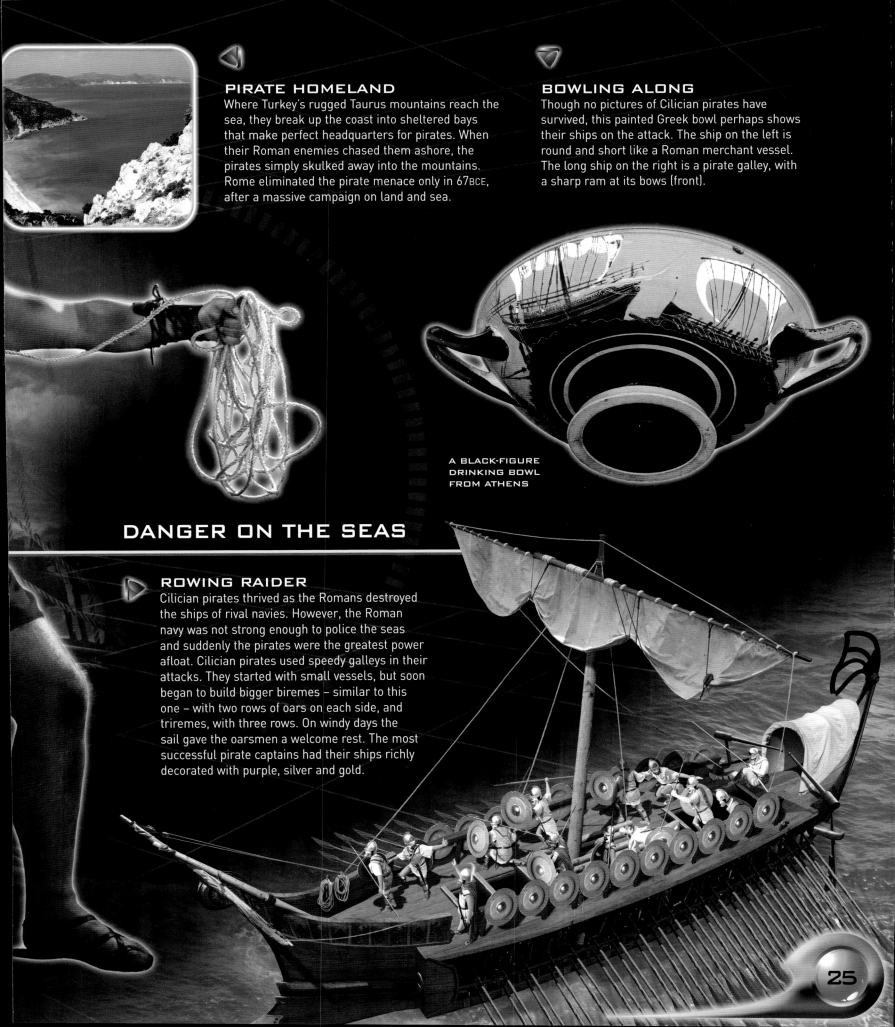

PIRATE HOMELAND

Where Turkey's rugged Taurus mountains reach the sea, they break up the coast into sheltered bays that make perfect headquarters for pirates. When their Roman enemies chased them ashore, the pirates simply skulked away into the mountains. Rome eliminated the pirate menace only in 67BCE, after a massive campaign on land and sea.

BOWLING ALONG

Though no pictures of Cilician pirates have survived, this painted Greek bowl perhaps shows their ships on the attack. The ship on the left is round and short like a Roman merchant vessel. The long ship on the right is a pirate galley, with a sharp ram at its bows (front).

A BLACK-FIGURE
DRINKING BOWL
FROM ATHENS

DANGER ON THE SEAS

ROWING RAIDER

Cilician pirates thrived as the Romans destroyed the ships of rival navies. However, the Roman navy was not strong enough to police the seas and suddenly the pirates were the greatest power afloat. Cilician pirates used speedy galleys in their attacks. They started with small vessels, but soon began to build bigger biremes – similar to this one – with two rows of oars on each side, and triremes, with three rows. On windy days the sail gave the oarsmen a welcome rest. The most successful pirate captains had their ships richly decorated with purple, silver and gold.

25

ROUNDSMAN

BALTIC PIRATE

ROUNDSMAN

THE ROUNDSMAN WINS

A GLANCE AT THE ROUNDSMAN'S SWORD TELLS THE BALTIC PIRATE ALL HE NEEDS TO KNOW. HIS OWN TWO-HANDED WEAPON IS HEAVIER AND LONGER, AND HE LEAPS FORWARD FOR WHAT HE THINKS WILL BE A QUICK VICTORY. BUT HE HASN'T BARGAINED FOR THE ROUNDSMAN'S MUSKETOON. LOADED WITH NAILS AND LEAD BALLS, IT DEALS THE VITALIENBRÜDER A FATAL BLOW. IT'S HARDLY A FAIR FIGHT, BUT AS LONG AS HE'S THE WINNER, THE ROUNDSMAN DOESN'T CARE.

THE BALTIC PIRATE IS BEATEN

ROUNDSMAN

BLACKBEARD PLAITED SMOULDERING FUSES INTO HIS HAIR TO FRIGHTEN HIS VICTIMS.

AS THE 17TH CENTURY ENDED, PIRATES DISCOVERED A NEW SOURCE OF BOOTY: INDIAN TREASURE SHIPS. BUT RAIDING THEM MEANT SAILING HALF WAY ROUND THE WORLD, ON A ROUTE NICKNAMED 'THE PIRATE ROUND'.

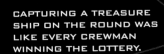

CAPTURING A TREASURE SHIP ON THE ROUND WAS LIKE EVERY CREWMAN WINNING THE LOTTERY.

WILLIAM KIDD BURYING HIS TREASURE

TREASURE VOYAGE

'Roundsmen' sailed 22,000km from New England (part of the modern-day USA) to the Indian Ocean in search of plunder. And what plunder it was! The gold and silver Thomas Tew took from an Indian ship in 1593 was worth £100,000 — the equivalent of £200 million today. Sent to round up the Roundsmen, William Kidd joined them instead. Other pirates of the time, who never joined the Roundsmen, could only envy them. Blackbeard is a famous example.

A PIRATE'S END

Despite their crimes, few Roundsmen were captured and punished. They drank themselves to death, died in action, were murdered or pardoned, or simply vanished. But a few paid a high price for their wickedness. William Kidd was arrested in America and sent to London for trial. Found guilty, he was hanged in 1701. His rotting corpse was displayed to discourage others from trying piracy.

ROUNDSMAN HENRY EVERY FLEW THIS FLAG WHEN HE ATTACKED.

'HANGING IN CHAINS' STOPPED PIRATES FROM GETTING A PROPER BURIAL.

PIRATE TRANSPORT

The small, fast ships favoured by Caribbean pirates were useless to Roundsmen. They needed much larger vessels to make the long voyage across the Atlantic and up Africa's east coast. William Kidd's *Adventure Galley*, for example, was a three-masted ship with mostly square sails, similar to this one. She had a crew of 150, and 34 cannons.

A PIRATE FLAG FLEW DURING ATTACKS.

STEADY ATLANTIC WINDS FILLED THE HUGE SQUARE SAILS.

33

BALTIC PIRATE

THE APPROACHING SAILS OF THE VITALIENBRÜDER PIRATES CAUSE PANIC ON A 14TH-CENTURY GERMAN MERCHANT SHIP. THE CREW KNOW THAT IF THEY RESIST ATTACK, THEY WILL DIE AT THE POINT OF A SWORD OR IN THE ICY BALTIC WAVES.

THESE CITY SEALS SHOW THE COG (SHIP) THAT WAS SO VITAL TO CITIES' LIVELIHOOD.

A SQUARE-SAILED PIRATE HULK APPROACHES ITS TARGET READY TO PLUNDER

BEARDED AND WILD-EYED, A BALTIC PIRATE WAS A TRULY FEARSOME FIGURE.

FIERCE RAIDERS

VILLAIN OR HERO?

Despite his murderous reputation, Baltic pirate captain Störtebeker (d.1402) is today a hero in his German homeland. He dealt fairly with his crew, and some believe that he gave his plunder to the poor. His name means 'down in one gulp', referring to a mug of beer.

STÖRTEBEKER'S STATUE IN MARIENHAFE, GERMANY

A SWORD AND DAGGER OF THE TYPE USED BY A VITALIENBRÜDER

"STÖRTEBEKER'S LAST WISH WAS THAT COMRADES HE COULD TOUCH AFTER HIS EXECUTION SHOULD BE SPARED. AFTER THE EXECUTIONER HAD STRUCK OFF HIS HEAD, STÖRTEBEKER'S HEADLESS CORPSE RAN OFF AND FREED 11 OF HIS COMPANIONS."

FROM SEAFARERS, MERCHANTS AND PIRATES IN THE MIDDLE AGES

PIRATES AND VICTIMS ALIKE USED SIMPLE WOODEN BOWS LIKE THIS IN THEIR BALTIC BATTLES.

A PIRATE'S END

Like these Baltic pirates, Störtebeker and his 73 crew were beheaded in Hamburg's main square. According to legend, after his death, workers found a solid gold core inside the mast of the pirate's ship. They used the gold to decorate the tip of Hamburg cathedral.

WEALTHY VICTIMS

The Vitalienbrüder targeted the shipping of the Hanse. This alliance of towns, which included the German city of Hamburg (below), stretched from the Netherlands to Poland. The piracy strangled Hanse trade in everything from salt to timber. Herrings – Hamburg's favourite food – were hit hardest.

VICTUALLING AND PIRACY

These pirates started their careers as privateers – sea raiders paid by Sweden's king. A rival imprisoned the king in 1389, but the city of Stockholm remained loyal to him, and was besieged. The privateers supplied Stockholm with victuals (food), earning themselves gratitude, and the nickname Vitalienbrüder (victual brothers). But popularity went to their heads, and they began raiding Baltic towns and shipping in their square-sailed hulks. They were rounded up and executed in 1402.

POWER BAR

VS

PICAROON

1. TURBAN-STYLE HAT

2. PAIR OF PISTOLS

3. CUTLASS

4. BOARDING AXE

5. FASHIONABLE LEATHER SHOES WITH SILVER BUCKLE

1720CE

DATA FILE

FEW FEMALES FOLLOWED THE PIRATE'S TRADE IN THE 18TH-CENTURY CARIBBEAN. THOSE WHO DID WERE FEARLESS. A PAIR OF THEM FOUGHT ALMOST ALONE WHEN THEIR SHIP WAS ATTACKED. THEY SHOUTED TO MALE COMRADES COWERING BELOW TO '...FIGHT LIKE MEN, OR DIE LIKE DOGS'.

PICK A WEAPON

CUTLASS
The cutlass's short blade makes it a good choice for combat on ships. A longer blade might catch in the rigging during a deck battle.

FLINTLOCKS
Don't rely too much on these pistols. They fire just once – or not at all if the powder is damp. A pair is the minimum: some pirates carry six.

BOARDING AXE
This cuts shrouds and stays, bringing down the ship's masts. With a heavy blade and spike, it's an awesome attack weapon, too.

ADD STAMINA

FOOD AND DRINK
Turned on its back, a turtle is helpless and stays alive for a week. It's delicious barbecued: wash down with jugs of spiced rum.

FIRST AID
Tropical diseases are more of a threat than violence. You could try raiding another ship for its medicine chest, but there are no real cures.

ADVICE
The pirates' code punishes those who desert the ship. When you're in a tight fix, comrades must answer your calls for help.

MAKE YOUR MOVE

FIRE!
Save your scarce pistol balls until you are sure you can't miss.

CLUB
Damp powder makes flintlocks misfire. Use them as clubs if they do.

CHOP
Make the most of your height: raise your cutlass high to inspire fear.

FREEBOOTER

YANG-FEI

YANG-FEI

THE BIGGEST PIRATE FLEET THE WORLD HAS EVER KNOWN CONTROLLED CHINESE SEAS 200 YEARS AGO. ITS CREWS WERE FEARLESS, AND EXPERT AT BLACKMAIL, TORTURE AND TERRORISM. THEIR LEADER, CHING I SAO, WAS A MATCH FOR ANY MAN.

JUNKS WERE MORE ADVANCED THAN EUROPEAN SHIPS.

YANG-FEI

THE FREEBOOTER HAS LOST

THE YANG-FEI WINS

WARY OF AN OPPONENT ARMED WITH PISTOLS, THE YANG-FEI HESITATES. THIS BOOSTS THE CONFIDENCE OF THE PICAROON, WHO SWAGGERS FORWARDS AND FOOLISHLY FIRES BOTH HER FLINTLOCKS TOGETHER. ONE MISFIRES; THE OTHER IS POORLY AIMED. AS THE PICAROON DROPS THE NOW-USELESS GUNS, THE YANG-FEI SEIZES HER CHANCE AND, WITH HER TWO HEAVY YAO-TAO BLADES, CUTS HER DOWN. A CRUSHING VICTORY FOR THE CHINESE PIRATE!

 PIRATE HUNTERS

CHING I SAO

When her husband, the admiral of the Red Flag fleet, died in 1807, Ching I Sao took command of his fleet of 300 junks. She introduced strict rules: anyone disobeying orders or hiding booty was beheaded. Deserters merely lost their ears. Like other female pirates in the fleet, Ching I fought when she needed to. This astonished Europeans, who read about her in trashy magazines (right).

CRUSHING THE PIRATES

Ching I surrendered in 1810 after rivalries split her fleet, but this did not end the threat of piracy around China's coast. Thirty years later the pirates damaged the valuable trade in the addictive drug opium, which British merchants were selling to China. To protect the trade, the British sent new-fangled steam battleships to hunt down the pirate junks. This painting shows British East India Company ships destroying pirate junks in Anson's Bay, China, in 1841.

ADD STAMINA

JUNK SAILORS

Though Ching I's Red Flag fleet had some huge battleships, most of the 300 or so ships were smaller. 12m-long junks like this one had crews of up to 200, and were armed with one or two dozen cannons. Captains and their families had a cabin at the stern; crews and their families shared the rat-infested hold.

FROM 1805, THE PIRATES OF THE SOUTH CHINA SEA WERE ORGANIZED INTO SIX FLEETS, EACH NAMED AFTER THE COLOURS OF THEIR FLAGS. THIS FLAG IS DEDICATED TO THE GODDESS T'IEN HOU, THE CALMER OF STORMS.

THE YANG-FEI DEMANDED MONEY FROM SEASHORE VILLAGERS WITH NOTES LIKE THESE.

THE YANG-FEI

Called yang-fei or 'sea bandits' by the Chinese officials who tried to stop them, the pirates attacked ships they knew they could easily capture. They crept up silently on their victims, and swarmed aboard, fighting in close combat with hand weapons. Though they had firearms, these were mainly used for show: sharp steel blades did the real work.

YANG-FEI MIGHT SPEND THEIR WHOLE LIVES AT SEA.

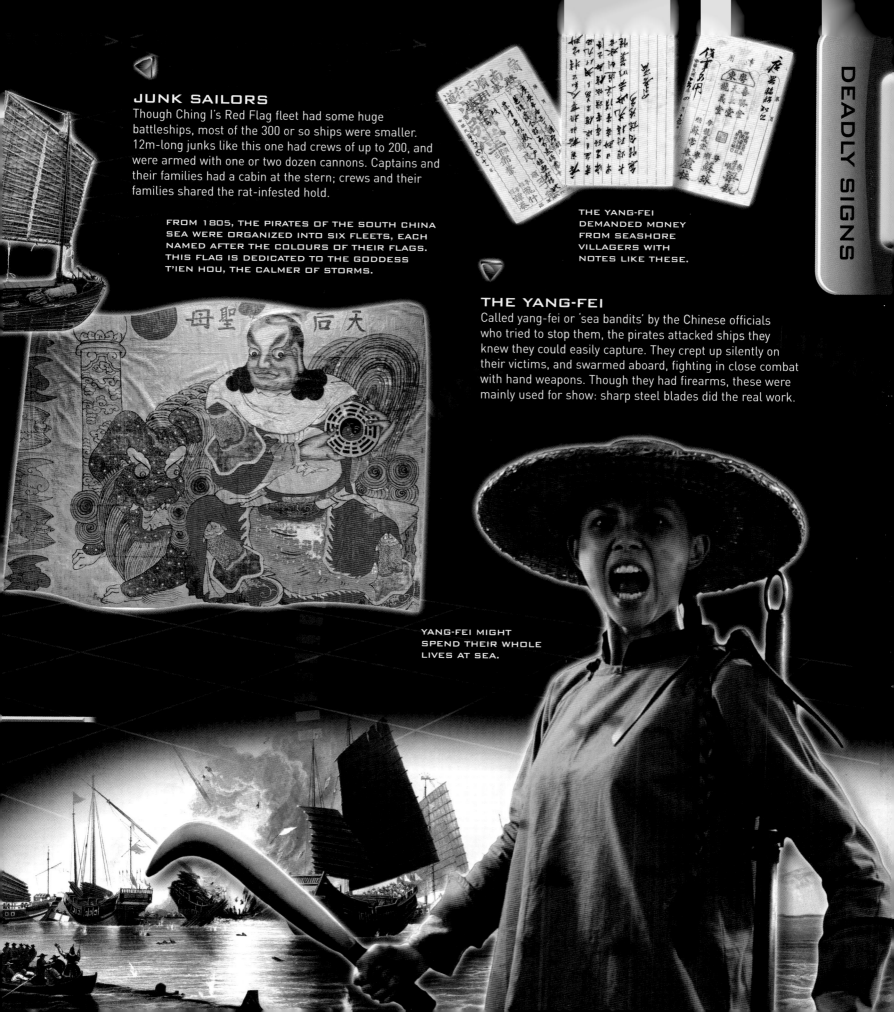

SWORDS, GUNS AND GRENADES

As well as flintlock pistols and short swords, Caribbean pirates used primitive pottery grenades. Their destructive power was small: they were most useful as smoke bombs to spread chaos during an attack.

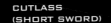

CUTLASS
(SHORT SWORD)

FLINTLOCK
PISTOLS

GRENADE
MADE OF
POTTERY

FREEBOOTER

MOST OF TODAY'S PIRATE STORIES ARE BASED ON THE GANGS WHO CRUISED THE CARIBBEAN AND BAHAMAS IN THE EARLY 18TH CENTURY. THESE ROWDY, DANGEROUS CREWS INCLUDED A COUPLE OF WOMEN PIRATES: MARY READ AND ANNE BONNY.

SWANNING AROUND

Though real female pirates were rare, writers cannot resist including them in their stories. In the *Pirates of the Caribbean* films, Keira Knightley plays pirate recruit Elizabeth Swann.

"NO PERSON THAT WAS AMONGST (THE PIRATES) WAS MORE READY TO UNDERTAKE ANY THING THAT WAS HAZARDOUS THAN (MARY READ) AND ANNE BONNY."
A GENERAL HISTORY OF THE PYRATES by CAPTAIN CHARLES JOHNSON (1724)

ON THE ATTACK

Pirates of fiction, such as these villains from *The Curse of the Black Pearl*, fight pitched battles on board vast men-of-war. Real pirate ships of the time were usually much smaller, and their raids less dramatic. Most of those targeted by pirates surrendered without a fight. Some willingly joined the crews of their attackers.

PIRATES LAUNCH THEMSELVES ONTO THEIR VICTIM SHIP.

MARY READ READY TO FIGHT

ANNE BONNY WITH HER PISTOL DRAWN

CALICO JACK'S SKULL-AND-CUTLASS FLAG

MARY AND ANNE

The most famous of all women pirates, Mary Read and Anne Bonny, sailed with 'Calico' Jack Rackham. Their cruise was a failure, and they were captured in 1720. Rackham's crew was tried and sentenced to death, but the women avoided hanging because they were pregnant. In sensational portraits the pair exposed their breasts; in fact they took care to dress like men.

SPEEDY SLOOP

Rackham and his crew sailed a sloop, probably a lot like this one. Sloops were fast, particularly with the wind behind them, and they could sail in shallow waters where bigger ships would run aground. They were not suitable for long ocean voyages, but this hardly mattered, for Calico Jack rarely raided far from land.

VIKING RAIDER

BARBARY CORSAIR

CORSAIR

THE CORSAIR WINS

THE VIKING IS USED TO FIGHTING CRUDELY ARMED MOBS AND RAIDING DEFENCELESS COASTAL PORTS. HE RELIES ON SHOCK AND AWE TO INTIMIDATE HIS OPPONENT. THE AZAP, HOWEVER, IS A SEASONED, DISCIPLINED FIGHTER, AND HE SPOTS HIS FOE'S WEAKNESSES. HIS SCIMITAR IS LIGHTER AND FASTER THAN THE VIKING'S HEAVIER SWORD, AND SOON HAS THE UPPER HAND. SWIFT CUTS TO THE VIKING'S UNPROTECTED LEGS BRING HIM DOWN AND PUT HIM AT THE CORSAIR'S MERCY.

THE VIKING HAS LOST

LONG-HANDLED TEBER FIGHTING AXE

CORSAIR

YELLING TERRIBLE CRIES OF HATRED, AN AZAP MARINE IS A TERRIFYING FOE. FIGHTING FOR THE MUSLIM RULERS OF AFRICA'S BARBARY COAST, HE CAPTURES CHRISTIAN GALLEYS, ENSLAVES THEIR CREWS AND RANSOMS WEALTHY PASSENGERS.

DECORATED NIMCHA SCIMITAR

SLENDER GALLEY

Barbary corsairs raided in sleek galleys (rowed ships). Scraped clean of barnacles and waxed for speed, they cruised the Mediterranean from the 15th century to 1830. When the wind blew, triangular sails powered the ships along, but on still days Christian slaves pulled on the huge oars. When the galleys were close enough to their victims, the elite Azap fighters swarmed aboard in overwhelming numbers.

BURNING SLAVES
ALIVE ON BLAZING
FIRES

CRUCIFYING SLAVES
ON WOOD CROSSES

ENTOMBING LIVE
SLAVES INSIDE
WALLS

CITIES OF SLAVERY

MUSLIM CHIEFS CALLED BEYS COMMANDED THE PIRATES FROM
THE BARBARY CITIES OF ALGIERS, TUNIS AND TRIPOLI. CAPTIVE
CHRISTIANS LIVED IN THE CITIES' SLAVE PRISONS UNTIL THEIR
FAMILIES PAID FOR THEIR FREEDOM. CHRISTIAN STORIES OF
TORTURED CAPTIVES (ABOVE) WERE MOSTLY INVENTIONS.

OTTOMAN SULTAN

The Barbary cities were distant parts of
the Ottoman Empire. Starting in 14th
century Turkey, Ottoman sultans (rulers)
such as Amurath III (1546–1595) spread
their rule and Muslim religion to vast
areas of Europe, Asia and Africa.

MALTA

As Ottoman galleys battled for control of
the Mediterranean, the island of Malta
was a stronghold of rival Christian
power. In 1565 Malta's defenders, the
Knights Hospitaller, fought off a
massive Ottoman attack from their
Fort St Angelo on the island.

DRAGUT REIS

Dragut Reis (1485–1565) commanded
Ottoman pirate galleys with such skill
that he became Bey of Tripoli, and
later Governor of the Mediterranean.
He died in the unsuccessful battle to
capture Malta.

VIKING RAIDER

SWEEPING ASHORE AT LIGHTNING SPEED, VIKING RAIDERS TERRIFIED THEIR VICTIMS. THE FIERCE NORSEMEN PLUNDERED SACRED TREASURE TROVES. THEY ENSLAVED YOUNG MEN AND WOMEN, AND DRAGGED AWAY VALUABLE CATTLE AND HORSES.

'SPECTACLED' HELMET PROTECTS THE EYES

DISPLAY OF SKILL
Vikings were not just crude warriors. In their homelands, many lived by farming or were skilled at crafts. Norse metalwork was spectacular. This 11th-century golden weather vane, used on a ship, has a lace-like pattern with a writhing beast at the centre.

A RECONSTRUCTION OF A VIKING LONGSHIP

ON THE ATTACK
Viking piracy began at the end of the eighth century with attacks on England. The raiders sailed from Scandinavia in longships: light, flexible vessels powered by both oars and woollen sails. Though warlike raiding continued for nearly three centuries, some later Viking journeys had more peaceful aims of settlement and trade. The Norsemen sailed deep into Russia, south to the Mediterranean, and even as far as North America.

A MODERN RE-ENACTMENT OF A VIKING ATTACK

PICTURE-BOOK TERROR

The raids of the 'godless' Vikings shocked Christian Europeans, as recorded in letters and hand-illustrated books. English scholar Alcuin wrote that 'Never before has such terror appeared in Britain from a pagan race, nor was it thought that such an inroad from the sea could be made.'

BERSERKERS

The most feared Viking warrior was the berserker, as depicted in this statue. The god Odin taught berserkers magic so they could blunt their enemy's swords and stop their javelins in flight. Before combat, they worked themselves up into a frenzy of rage which doubled their strength and made them unable to feel pain.

VIKING ARMOUR

Vikings wear horned helmets only in bad movies! Most wore plain domed helmets, of leather or metal. Some Vikings also protected their upper bodies with chain-mail vests – if they could afford them. This metal helmet, found in a Norwegian burial mound, is so beautifully crafted that it must have belonged to a wealthy chief.

A VIKING AXE WAS BOTH TOOL AND WEAPON

FIRST RAID

Holy Island, or Lindisfarne, lies just off England's windy north-east coast. It was the site of the Vikings' first major raid in 793. The Norsemen attacked the island because there was a monastery there. They knew they would find valuable church treasures, and that the monks would be almost defenceless. After a second raid 82 years later, the monks fled to the mainland with the sacred bones of St Cuthbert (which apparently did not interest the Vikings)! Today Lindisfarne monastery (left) is a beautiful ruin.

FIVE VICTORS

OUR PIRATE COMBATS ARE A FANTASY: THESE ROGUES NEVER MET IN REAL LIFE. SO HOW CAN WE TELL WHO WOULD WIN EACH FIGHT – AND WHO, OF ALL TEN, WOULD BE THE ULTIMATE VICTOR? WE CAN'T KNOW FOR CERTAIN, BUT INTELLIGENT GUESSWORK IS POSSIBLE. PIRATES MADE SURE THEY WOULD TRIUMPH BEFORE THEY STARTED A BATTLE. THEY TOOK CARE THAT THEY WOULD OUTNUMBER, OUT-SAIL AND OUT-GUN THEIR VICTIMS. BUT OUR COMBATANTS FIGHT HAND-TO-HAND, WITHOUT HELP. SUPERIOR WEAPONS MAY GIVE ONE AN ADVANTAGE, BUT SKILL, STRENGTH AND LUCK ARE JUST AS IMPORTANT.

WINNER: ROUNDSMAN

Firearms, of course, give the roundsman an unfair advantage over his foe from the Baltic. However, even without a gun he is hard to beat. Toughened by long sea voyages, his whole way of life is a high-stakes gamble – and he never even considers losing.

WINNER: BUCCANEER

Without firing a shot, the buccaneer has the edge over his Cilician foe. Rough living has made him muscular; and with his butchery skills he can place a blade where it will do maximum damage.

WINNER: PRIVATEER

With steel weapons, and practice in pitched battles, the privateer has a head start over his Sea People adversary, who has a bronze sword and is more used to unopposed raiding.

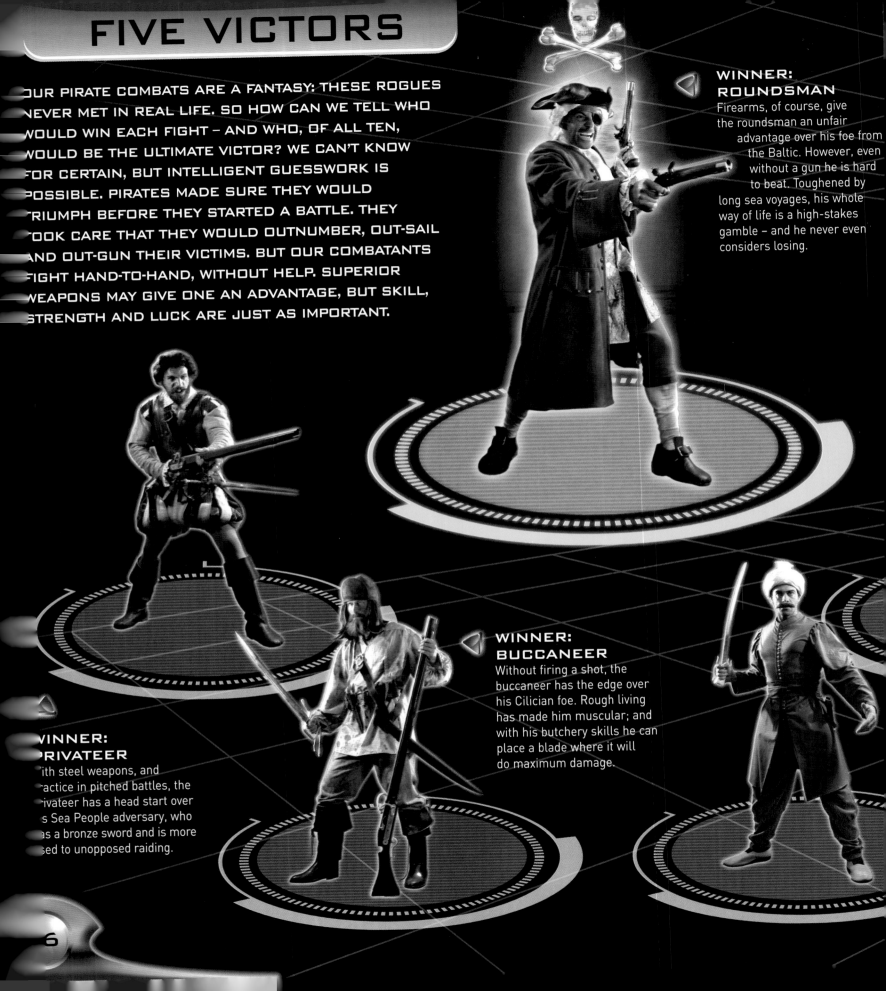

6

ROUNDSMAN

THE ROUNDSMAN CAN CONFIDENTLY TAKE ON ANY OF THE OTHER VICTORS. HE REGULARLY ATTACKS CREWS THAT PUT UP A STUBBORN DEFENCE. HE IS USED TO THE HARDSHIPS OF MONTHS AT SEA. HIS WEAPONS ARE THE BEST AND HE MAINTAINS THEM CAREFULLY. MOST OF ALL, HE IS DETERMINED. NOTHING AND NO ONE CAN STAND BETWEEN HIM AND A FORTUNE.

ULTIMATE VICTOR

WINNER: YANG-FEI
Facing a taller opponent with pistols, the yang-fei seems to stand little chance. But the freebooter's over-confidence and unreliable weapons are her undoing. The yang-fei ruthlessly exploits her stroke of luck to grab a well-deserved victory.

WINNER: BARBARY CORSAIR
Discipline is the key to victory in the battle when Viking and corsair clash. The Norseman is an unruly scrapper who aims to terrify his victim. This doesn't unnerve the corsair, who is drilled in efficient fighting technique.

WINNER HEAD TO TOE

PISTOL – deadly when it works, and the roundsman makes sure it does by keeping his powder dry.

SWORD – stolen from a wealthy victim, this fine blade is better than anything he could afford to buy.

CLOTHING – though it offers little protection, it makes the roundsman look the dandy he believes he is.

MIND – roundsmen are ingenious in tracking and smart in attacking, and clever businessmen when it comes to selling plunder.

HEART – ruthless towards his foes, he treats his crews and allies honourably.

WE'VE FOUND OUR FIVE VICTORS AND OUR ULTIMATE
WINNER. BUT WOULD THINGS HAVE BEEN DIFFERENT IF
THE CONTESTS HAD BEEN BETWEEN DIFFERENT PAIRS?
WHAT DO YOU THINK? WHOSE WEAPONS ARE BEST?
WHO IS MOST SKILLED? WHO HAS THE MENTAL EDGE?

VIKING VS BUCCANEER

Seven centuries separate these two pirates, yet they
share a similar brawling style of fighting. The Viking
has the advantage of a shield with which to defend
himself, but the weight of his axe makes it slow to
swing. Is the buccaneer quick enough to land a blow
with his long knife before the Viking's axe falls?

WINNER: YOU DECIDE...

CILICIAN VS YANG-FEI

If strength and weight decided every battle, the
Cilician would win easily, for he towers over his
female adversary. Nevertheless, the outcome is not
a certainty. The yang-fei is the more agile pirate, and
the Cilician is very wary of slashes from her long
ch'ang-ping tao. It could be a long duel!

WINNER: YOU DECIDE...

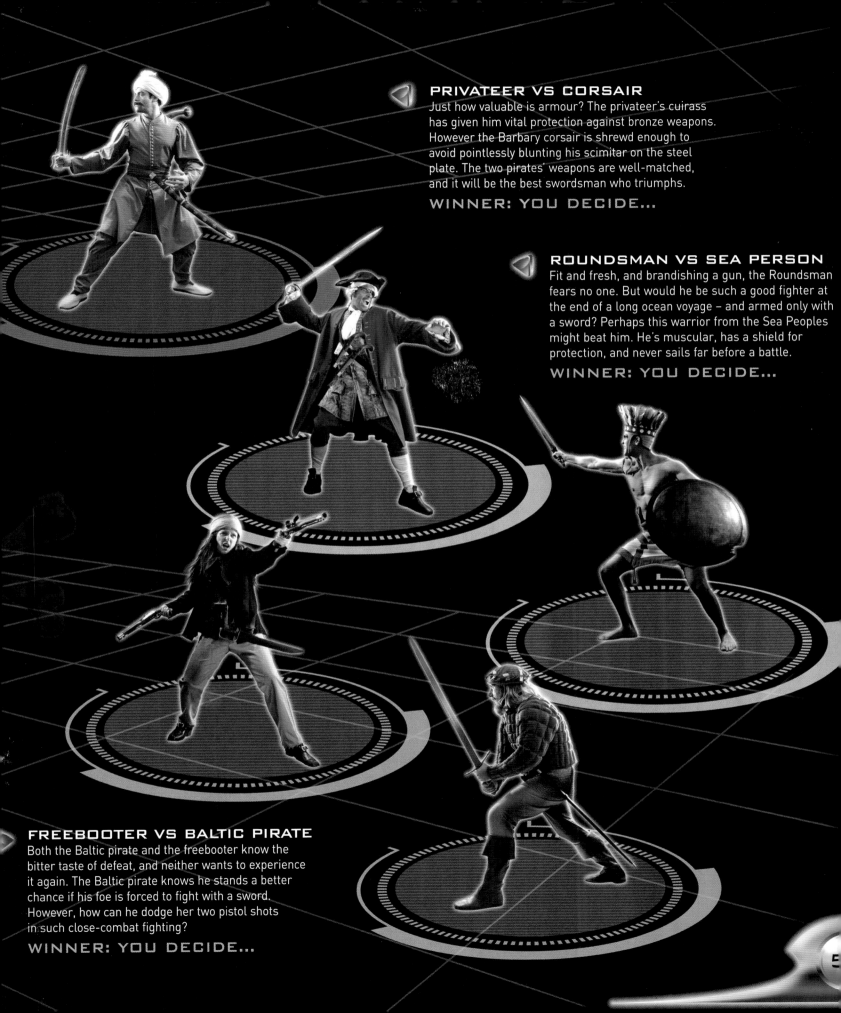

PRIVATEER VS CORSAIR

Just how valuable is armour? The privateer's cuirass has given him vital protection against bronze weapons. However the Barbary corsair is shrewd enough to avoid pointlessly blunting his scimitar on the steel plate. The two pirates' weapons are well-matched, and it will be the best swordsman who triumphs.

WINNER: YOU DECIDE...

ROUNDSMAN VS SEA PERSON

Fit and fresh, and brandishing a gun, the Roundsman fears no one. But would he be such a good fighter at the end of a long ocean voyage – and armed only with a sword? Perhaps this warrior from the Sea Peoples might beat him. He's muscular, has a shield for protection, and never sails far before a battle.

WINNER: YOU DECIDE...

FREEBOOTER VS BALTIC PIRATE

Both the Baltic pirate and the freebooter know the bitter taste of defeat, and neither wants to experience it again. The Baltic pirate knows he stands a better chance if his foe is forced to fight with a sword. However, how can he dodge her two pistol shots in such close-combat fighting?

WINNER: YOU DECIDE...

BALTIC PIRATE

ALLIANCE An agreement of friendship between people, families, tribes or countries, so that they can together attack an enemy that threatens both of them.

AMBER A rare kind of hardened tree resin that looks like clear yellow plastic. It is used in jewellery.

BALTIC An inland sea that separates Norway and Sweden from the rest of Northern Europe.

CHAIN MAIL A kind of armour made from thousands of small metal rings, linked together to form a flexible coat.

COG A small ship with a square sail, built out of oak in Northern Europe from the tenth century.

HANSE A 13th–17th century trading alliance of towns in lands bordering the coasts of Northern Europe. It included Lübeck, Hamburg and Cologne (in modern-day Germany), Riga (in Latvia) and Danzig (in Poland).

MERCHANT Someone who earns money by buying things and selling at a higher price.

VITALIENBRÜDER A group of pirates who supplied the Swedish city of Stockholm with food when it was surrounded by a hostile army in the 14th century.

BARBARY CORSAIR

AZAP A Turkish volunteer soldier fighting for the Ottoman empire, often forming part of the fighting force on a Barbary corsair.

BEY The ruler of a Muslim city or region under the Ottoman empire.

CORSAIR A pirate ship licensed by the Ottoman empire, or a pirate sailing one of these ships.

CRUCIFY To execute someone by fixing them to a tall wooden cross.

GALLEY A large ship powered mainly by oars.

JANISSARIES Muslim soldiers, recruited as boys from Christian parents in the Ottoman empire.

OTTOMANS The powerful Turkish rulers who controlled the region around the Black Sea and eastern Mediterranean for 400 years from the 16th century.

PAGAN A name given by Christians to those who do not share their religion.

RANSOM A fee paid for the release of a wealthy prisoner.

SCIMITAR A short curved sword, sharpened on just one edge, used especially by Turks and Persians.

BUCCANEER

BACKWOODS A wild, untamed area beyond farmland or towns.

BARREL (of gun) A long straight tube that directs the bullet or ball accurately towards the target when the gun is fired.

BOUCANIERS/ BUCCANEERS 17th-century hunters, and later pirates, on Hispaniola. The name comes from the boucan (barbecue) that they used to cook and preserve meat.

FUSE (of gun) A slow-burning cord used to set fire to the gunpowder in a crude, early gun.

GAME Wild birds and animals hunted for food.

HELMSMAN The sailor who steers a ship.

HISPANIOLA The old name for the second-biggest Caribbean island, now Haiti and the Dominican Republic.

MATCHLOCK Simple gun fired using a fuse.

MATELOT A buccaneer's close friend and hunting partner.

RIGGING Ropes used to support and control the masts, yards and sails of a ship.

CILICIAN

BIREME A galley with two rows of oars, one above the other.

BOWS The back-end of a ship.

CILICIA An old name for the part of southern Turkey near the Mediterranean sea.

GLADIATOR A slave trained to fight in combats staged for the entertainment of Roman people.

GLADIUS The name for a sword in Latin, the Roman language.

GRAPPLING HOOK A three- or four-pronged metal hook with a rope attached, thrown to fix the rope to a ship or wall.

IMPROVISED Made from objects intended for a quite different use – for example, a farming tool or piece of ship's equipment used as a weapon.

PRAEDO The Latin word for a pirate or bandit.

PUGIO A Roman dagger.

SLAVE A captive person bought and sold as a possession, without the rights that free people enjoy, and made to work without pay.

TRIREME A galley with three rows of oars, one above the other.

FREEBOOTER

COMRADE A companion, close friend or fellow pirate.

CUTLASS A short sword, perhaps invented by buccaneers, and later used by navies.

FLINTLOCK A simple, one-shot gun, fired by the spark from a spring-loaded flint (a glassy stone).

FREEBOOTER Another word for a pirate.

GRENADE A small bomb, thrown by hand.

MAN-OF-WAR A large wooden battleship powered by sails.

PICAROON A pirate, slave trader or the ship they command.

RIGGING The ropes used to support and control the masts, yards and sails of a ship.

SHROUDS Ropes supporting a ship's masts, stopping them from swaying port and starboard (left and right).

SLOOP A small, fast ship with a single mast, used by 18th-century pirates.

STAYS Supporting ropes that stop a ship's masts from swaying fore and aft (forwards and backwards).

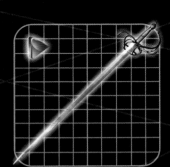

SWORDS
The shape of these long blades depends on their use – slender and sharply pointed for thrusting, or heavier, wider blades sharpened on one or both edges for slashing.

AXES
Adapted from simple tools, axes could make devastating weapons at sea. Their heavy blades broke bones and caused terrible wounds, or cut ropes supporting a ship's masts.

GUNS
Used with care, these firearms could hit distant targets. Pirates often lacked the discipline to fire them accurately, using them instead to frighten their foes.

PRIVATEER

ADMIRAL The commander of a fleet or navy.

CALIVER A small flintlock gun with a long barrel, fired from the shoulder.

CANNON A large gun, too heavy to lift, fired from a stand.

DOUBLET A tight-fitting piece of clothing like a jacket, worn between the 14th and 18th centuries.

MAN-OF-WAR A large wooden battleship powered by sails.

NAVY The fleet of ships and their crew that a country uses to control shipping and wage war at sea.

PARRY To fend off a blow or sword-cut in a fight.

PARTISAN A long spear with a triangular blade at its tip.

PRIVATEER A sea-captain carrying a license from a ruler or government that allows them to attack enemy ships in wartime.

RAPIER A slender, pointed sword.

STEEL A strong metal alloy (mixture) of iron and carbon.

VOLLEY Gunfire from many hand-held weapons, all firing at once.

ROUNDSMAN

ALBATROSS A very large soaring bird of the world's southern oceans. Pirates and other sailors thought a ship lucky if an albatross followed it, and believed that killing one would bring bad luck.

BARREL (of gun) A gun's long straight tube, which directs the bullet or ball accurately towards the target when the gun is fired.

FLINTLOCK A simple, one-shot gun, loaded with a lead ball and fired by the spark from a spring-loaded flint (a glassy stone).

NEW ENGLAND The extreme north-east corner of what is now the United States, where European people first settled in the 16th century.

SCURVY A deadly disease, suffered by sailors on voyages longer than about six weeks, and caused by a lack of vitamin C in fruit and vegetables. Scurvy caused blotchy skin, loss of teeth, and eventually death.

TRIGGER The control lever on a gun that, when pulled back with the finger, fires the weapon at the target.

SEA PEOPLES

BRONZE A metal made by mixing two other metals – copper and tin.

IVORY The precious, decorative and easily carved teeth or tusks of elephants.

MURAL A picture painted directly onto the surface of a wall. Murals decorated the tombs of wealthy ancient Egyptians.

PELESET An ancient name for the people of Palestine – the Philistines of the Bible.

PHARAOH The name for a king in ancient Egypt.

PHOENICIA An ancient country (modern-day Lebanon).

PLUNDER To steal valuable goods using force, or the goods obtained in this way.

SACRIFICE Killing an animal or person as part of a religious celebration.

SEA PEOPLES A name the ancient Egyptians gave to the seafaring people of the Eastern Mediterranean who raided their coasts more than 3000 years ago.

TOMB-TEMPLE The temple built close to an ancient Egyptian tomb, in honour of the dead person.

PISTOLS
The short barrels of these hand-held weapons meant they could hit only nearby targets. Their small size made them convenient for pirates, who commonly carried several.

SPEARS
Mounting a sharp point at the end of a long pole creates a dual-purpose weapon. Used for prodding, they kept an enemy away. Hurled, they had more power than arrows.

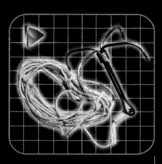

GRAPPLING HOOK
Curved and spiked, the prongs of a grappling hook are meant to tangle and catch as a rope anchor during boarding. Used for fighting they can tear, crush and injure.

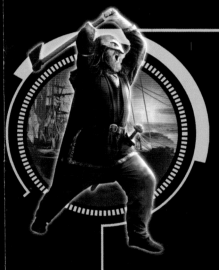

VIKING RAIDER

BERSERKERS Terrifying Viking warriors who worked themselves up into a furious frenzy before attacking.

CHAIN MAIL A kind of armour made from thousands of small metal rings, linked together to form a flexible coat.

LONGSHIP A long war galley with a square sail, used for raiding by Viking warriors.

MONASTERY A home and place of work and worship for monks: men who live simple lives devoted to God.

NORSEMEN People of Scandinavia before the spread of Christianity.

ODIN The most important of the Norse gods.

POMMEL A round knob fixed at the end of a sword handle to balance the blade.

RUNE A letter, usually cut in wood or stone, from the Viking alphabet.

STAFNBÚI The Viking name for the fighters at the front of a longship, who led the attack.

YANG-FEI

ADMIRAL The commander of a fleet or navy.

BILLHOOK A wide, heavy, hooked knife, traditionally used to trim hedges, and used by Chinese pirates as a weapon.

BLACKMAIL Using knowledge of an embarrassing or dangerous secret to force someone to pay money or do something they do not want to do.

BOOTY Valuable goods stolen by robbers or raiders.

CH'ANG-PING TAO A long, heavy sword carried on the shoulders and swung with both hands. Its name means 'knife carried on the shoulder'.

OPIUM A dangerous drug made from poppies, illegally sold to Chinese addicts by European countries in the 18th and 19th centuries.

PIKE A very long spear, sometimes three times as long as the soldier carrying it.

RANSOM Large fee paid for the release of a wealthy prisoner.

YAO-TAO A short, wide, hooked sword.